DARK MATTERS

Katharyn Howd Machan

FUTURECYCLE PRESS
www.futurecycle.org

Cover artwork, "Tricked You into Following Me" by Casey Landerkin; author photo by Carol Openshaw; cover and interior book design by Diane Kistner; Georgia text, Anagram and Georgia titling

Copyright © 2017 Katharyn Howd Machan
All Rights Reserved

Published by FutureCycle Press
Athens, Georgia, USA

ISBN 978-1-942371-40-3

for Alison Lurie

Contents

Path 7
Paws 9
My Beast 10
Dark Matters 11
Your Mother 12
Sonnet 13
Autism, 1954 14
What He Meant, the Miller 15
In His Fingers 16
Learning to Lie, the Nice Girl 17
Noir 18
After My Brother Stole Me Away 19
When Your Daughter-in-Law Hates Magic 20
The Women Who Write About Animals 21
My Granddaughter Hands Me a Gilded Box 22
Blackbird Bakery 23
Black 24
I Will Give You Flowers 25
Leda's Sister and the Geese 26
Helen 27
Penelope 28
The Feather of the Winter Owl 30
Prayer Sequence 31
An Account of My Disappearances 32
When Lilith Goes Out Dancing 34
End-of-Day 35
Old Women Crying on the Beach 36
Beneath the Tallest Live Oak 37
Acknowledgments

Path

> "I don't know what I want but I don't want this..."
> —Anonymous, in *PostSecret,* compiled by Frank Warren
> (ReganBooks, 2005)

He's the shadow in the leaves.
He carries a bag. It has claws.
All I have is my thin red sweater
and I can't ever pause.

When I was seven a carnival clown
tried to get me up to the stage
to toss my kisses into a hat
that sparkled with black diamonds.
"The little girl in the red sweater!"
he called, and gestured with glimmering gloves.
My mother urged me, but I shrank back,
and another little girl—in blue—got
to see her lips make rainbow candy.

My brother's ghost is a wisp of smoke.
I swam his ashes into the sea,
then changed into warm dry jeans
and my red sweater, tight on me.

When I was sixteen I knew a woman
ninety-two who liked to crochet.
I served her breakfast, cleaned her room,
and listened to her stories of France,
how she went to balls and wore real emeralds
and how glad she was she could remember
all this way across the ocean
with others who were old. She gave me
a red sweater when we said goodbye.

Maybe he's a wolf in a fairy tale.
Maybe he's a doctor who wants me dead.
I can't quite see in my red sweater
no matter how often I turn my head.

At thirty-five I went to Sardinia
and easily touched a goddess's face.
The harbor made me shake in awe.
Right next to magnificent Cagliari

small ancient homes were open, too,
and women somber from head to toe
herded their goats and sheep nearby.
I didn't know that I was pregnant
but I wore a red sweater inside my chest.

He slyly moves when I start walking.
Moonlight's never quite enough.
What time is it? What time, Mr. Fox?
My sweater's ragged at its red cuff.

Paws

> "Keep talking. How did the story go?"
> —Sara Eliza Johnson in "Märchen"

It's always the wolf. Count on it.
Hunger just outside the door
and the distant church bell ringing.
Little girl in a crimson cap,
small boy sneaking out through the gate,
young pigs behind flimsy walls.
Even the brother and sister, abandoned,
would have been swallowed by shining eyes
if the witch hadn't taken them in.

The oldest stories are the oldest stories
until they turn true again,
each one a shard of mirror
piercing our softest flesh.
Monks may sing in midnight choir,
but how far does their music reach?
Look to the basket, the swallowed duck,
the straw and the sticks shuttered tight.
The wolf grins. Bet your life.

I haven't lived more than sixty years
without learning a tale or three.
Where do my poems come from?
Told to lie still, shut up, keep secrets,
dark weight like a rat on my brain,
and me just one of the many many
praying the wolf will be caught and cut
or shot or burned or boiled to death
so he'll never howl again.

My Beast

walks to the cupboard, reaches in,
drinks too much red wine and vomits
words about a treacherous mother
who smoked cigarettes, wore thin high heels,
stayed up nights sipping hard-core whiskey

from a lipstick-crimsoned glass.
Walks miles and thinks the world is flat
as music from a broken piano
abandoned when the composer died
alone in a small blue room.

Dresses in a ragged cape aflame
with shivering orange-yellow candles
that give no heat nor light but never
cease their tiny birthday burning.
Rapes my daughter with a smile

on his face, teeth pumpkin-rotting black.
Hands my granddaughter a smooth
scarlet cap, a perfect white rose,
a key he tells her she must never use
to open the door to his wild crooked heart.

Dark Matters

It's a simple story—
no, it is not:
just because so many know it
doesn't mean it's clear.

A girl enters a shadowed forest,
leaving warm sunlight behind.
Her mother is long gone from her.
Her father's busy with his ax.
Her grandmother waits in a blue room
grinding bones to feed tight violets.
Her brother—well, her brother: the tale
begins with the spider in his heart
helplessly growing round and hard
with venom poised within its bite
to poison the whole family.

Call him Hansel with no pocket for stones,
no fingers to crumble dry bread,
no little white cat grinning on the roof,
his sister a threat to love.
His mother the witch
with her hard crimson nails
is his wife, is his life,
is a hard demon's tail.

His sister hopes feared gray-haired Gothel
can keep her free of the prince's touch,
but crone doesn't see
and crone doesn't know
until she knows too much—
then beats the girl with a naked hand
crying crying crying out loud
you are filth   you are dirt
we have never loved you

Cinderella looks on and stares,
denying all that's black and strange:
she's got crystal bottles swearing
all the choices she has made
are for the good of fairy tales
shaping a sure steady castle
to keep its children safe.

Your Mother

for Carla

I saw Kennedy get shot she says
when you were a baby at home.
I took you to Woodstock she says
and you peed where nude people swam.
And now you stitch wings to old keys
and shape giant birds of paper?
You get paid for making art
about books the whole world reads?
You tell your children you must stay
as far from me as you're able?
In the voice beyond her voice
you hear your young self silent.
In secret words she tries to swear
she never let him touch you.
I was there in Dallas she says.
I wore tie-dye on Yasgur's farm.
How could you ever believe I would let
anyone do you harm?

Sonnet

> "Little Song, little Song, can you speak about Wrong?"
> —Connie Willis

Especially when Father has no wife.
Especially when you learned as a child
a girl must be obedient, not wild,
and dedicate to him your lesser life.

Especially when Father holds a knife.
Especially when in his voice kept mild
you find your need for questioning reviled
as evil discord, wanton devil's strife.

You know you cannot leave, for only he
can ever love you as you are and were,
the worthless one whose deeds must never be
more than his silent words say can occur.

Especially when Father nods goodnight,
picks up the blade, turns out the bedside light.

Autism, 1954

He's the fairy tale boy, the mute, the giant,
the troll that growls beneath the bridge,
the snake that swallows maidens. All

his life he's feared his tongue's on fire,
his fingers tumbling every brick
he's tried to pile up high. *Wolf!*

the trembling peasants scream, pitchforks
toward his eyes. His beard is blue,
his feet are hooves: much better when he

dies.

What He Meant, the Miller

When he said deep in his cups
his daughter could turn straw to gold
he was leering, he was bragging
about the way he'd turned her bed
into his own pleasure, she thirteen
and afraid to say no with her mother

gone less than a year. A man has
needs, a man has wants, and him
so worn out by work! She looking
just like his dead wife and each night
an ache in his groin: brag of her, find
a husband eager for young smooth hips

glittering hot with wide welcome.
How could a drunk father even dream
the King would be told of his claim?
A baby already spinning inside and
the sharp dwarf watching, awaiting
his chance, ready to gamble his name.

In His Fingers

for Julia Bieber

the dry straw gleamed and smelled of summer
as he separated shaft from shaft
and fed them to the wooden wheel
rasping rasping in rapid whirl
while darkness swallowed time

the miller's daughter in her simple dress
sat near to watch with dreadful fear
and felt that she might choke on chaff
dust everywhere around his smile
that made no sound at all

gold spooled slick as a shining snake
and seemed to hiss against the night
as ravaged fields now cluttered stubble
held to silence where September's winds
blew far and wide a whispered name

Learning to Lie, the Nice Girl

says she found the flowers herself
right next to the path in a sudden patch
of sunlight between the high dark trees
that pointed the way to Granny's

she tells how they fit all orange and blue
between the sweet cakes and bottle of wine
her mother'd packed neatly in the curved basket
that just fit over her arm

she doesn't tell anyone of the wolf
who dallied with her on the soft crimson cape
before she stuffed it down his throat
and sat there watching him die

Noir

And if the prince is evil.
If his fingertips are dangerous

when he pries loose the golden slipper
from tar, from pitch, from wax.

Ochre waistcoat, mustard sleeves, thin
necktie in a saffron knot

below a bearded grin. If
every night he plucks black swans

and floats their feathers down the stream
that runs fast past his castle,

then chews their curved necks raw
to spit out their splintered bones,

laughing as he shouts the name
of the shining girl he'll seek and find

to marry, then cut off her feet
so she'll never dance again.

After My Brother Stole Me Away

I learned to lick honey off a thorn
and dew from underneath a clover,
tearing nothing, neither tongue nor leaf,
and growing strong as a forest doe
no hunter could ever shoot down.
He left me far from our mother's hearth
to die in the cold, held by hard magic
he'd taken at night from our father's harp

where it hung on the carved oaken door.
But my breath rose and touched the branches
and owls swooped low and foxes stepped
and together they saved me from black storm
to wake me in a bed of feathers
warm with white-tipped tails. Song
turned all shadows, dance whirled my light,
words beyond mere human words became

the reach of dawn. Never did I see again
the boy who longed to kill me. When he
was found dead with a tooth in his heart
and his fingers begging to God,
I was years away in summer, hands
stained with wild strawberries, red and
small and sweet to share, my mouth
full and smiling.

When Your Daughter-in-Law Hates Magic

Hide your spoons.
Mask your gingerbread

as cumin cookies, lemon loaf,
any scent that will put her off

what you offer to the world.
She must never know

how you saved that baby from the sting
of the tiny Mexican scorpion

or how you died on that cold beach
of the lake that shivered your name.

She's married now, to that warm son
you kept alive on your round breast.

Stay somber, quiet, staunch with grace.
When she turns her gaze away

you know you'll go dancing high
to tango with the moon's sharp curve:

your breath rising full and hard
as the broom your clear prayers ride.

The Women Who Write About Animals

The women who write about animals
carry pieces of night in their eyes.
They howl. They climb trees
and sharpen their claws on cool bark.
These women learned to dream
of roots and briars, the strength of green,
white sand along bright streams
for lettering secret runes.
They grew to understand fur.
They longed for rough tongues.
Now their poems see in the dark.
They go out walking on four legs
and fear nothing that walks on two.

My Granddaughter Hands Me a Gilded Box

full of Tarot cards that matter
now that she's with me, safe, alive,
out of the cave where gnarled trolls fester
in twisted shoes, in rotting gloves. Tell

me a fairy tale again, Babushka
her small mouth asks below blue eyes
mirror and mirror of all the women
I carry in my blood. And so I choose

King of Cups in his crimson thobe,
Knight of Pentacles green as dragons,
and one more from the bright stack's center,
The Hanging Man in chains and stars:

hero I know she will love one day
when they both burst loose from time's blue mountain
and wave to me where I'll be riding
far away on my good black horse.

Blackbird Bakery

Every pie's made with cinnamon
and every pie with its short crust whistles
because the woman of many aprons

presses little ceramic birds
just off center where the heat cooks best
strawberry, sweet peach, deep Dutch apple

to make the open beaks call joy
at gleaming golden brown perfection.
She lives alone and not alone

in this house almost made of gingerbread,
her years of stirring, mixing, spreading
alive as any fox-eyed children

she might have birthed to the world.
And nights, sometimes, when stars call down
a hundred small dark wings unfold

and take her flying through the forest
where she is sure her story began
on a thin path scattered with crumbs.

Black

as a belladonna eye.
As tiny feathers pulled from a crow
by two redwings guarding speckled

eggs slung from cattail reeds. As an
eyelash strummed with thick mascara
drifting down to a woman's hand that's

touched too many winters. Small goats
high on rocks off Skyros. Tangled hair
of the sailor hauling nets at dawn

after too much night with ouzo. Ink
forcing poems onto paper from trees
that once threw shadows for lean hounds

escaping blood sacrifice. Ground pepper
poured too fast from a thin tin box
into a tiny fox-shaped shaker, spilling

wildly wide near an empty bottle
of wine that cost too much. A piano
sold fast and hard by a widow

no matter how much a daughter has cried.
A leather satchel, left behind in an attic,
with all his dark music inside.

I Will Give You Flowers

red as boar's blood.
White as a handkerchief
a queen might give her only daughter
as a shield, a charm. a promise.
Yellow, too, like the tongue of a cow
stained with buttercups, marigolds
in a field where the fence is made of wire
and a young girl goes to hide.
Flowers are gathered into bouquets
and flowers are woven for crowns.
I'll give them to you from my own basket
curved into a crescent moon.
Purple as veins in a bent crone's hands.
Blue as eyes in a white cat's head.
And pink as ribbons a wandering child
might tug from her hair, tie to a tree,
hoping that fairies will find them and know
she's ready to join them, ready to flee.

Leda's Sister and the Geese

All the boys always wanted her, so
it was no surprise about the swan-
man, god, whatever he was. That day

I was stuck at home, as usual, while
she got to moon around the lake
supposedly picking lilies for dye. Think *I*

would have let some pair of wings catch me,
bury me under the weight of the sky?
She came home whimpering, whined out

the whole story, said she was "sore afraid"
she'd got pregnant. Hunh. "Sore"
I'll bet, the size she described, and

pregnant figures: no guess who'll get
to help her with the kid or, Hera forbid,
more than one (twins run in our damned

family). "Never you mind, dear," Mother said.
"Your sister will take on your chores."
Sure. As though I wasn't already doing

twice as many of my own. So now
I clean, I spin, I weave, I bake,
fling crusts to feed these birds I wish

to Hades every day; while she sits smug
in a wicker chair, and eats sweetmeats,
and combs and combs that ratty golden hair.

Helen

They say it was my face. No:
let me tell you about marriage.
Silences and swords, a stone house,
my women whispering around me
dull as bees. For years before he touched
our doorsill, I dreamt his voice;

the silver gifts he brought were tiny
mirrors of the girl I'd held inside
too long. Soon I turned willing hands
to weave for him, each thread a piece
of secret song. The peacock blue, the purple
heart of pansies, red a cry of sun

setting over unclimbed hills. *I asked
to go with him.* I knew he watched
me walk across cool tile, my feet
in sandals I yearned to kick away
so I could run to him unbound
by safe convention. Strange strong guest,

reluctant to offend the man he knew
I didn't love, whose hospitality
was heartless, rote, a hand that drops
coins in a beggar's cup without a glance.
One morning when the sun rose white
and helplessly again I moved to stand

beside him where the swans swim slow,
he took my hand in his and nodded *yes.*
All time burst to blossom and I
knew what it was to be the rose.
Swift ships, sting of salty air, my hair
wrapped around his fingers in the dark:

we could have lived forever in that place
of travel, seabirds wailing overhead,
the men around us eyeing me like some
pure stolen chance—how could they know?—and my
hopes free as any muscled gleaming fish
leaping higher than those blue and bitter waves.

Penelope

    after Adrienne Rich

The world remembers me for loving him:
sleeping chaste in Ithaca, my heart firm
as the living tree he carved for our bed.
Good Penelope! Faithful and cunning wife
to fool with woof and warp
the suitors who would claim
all that Odysseus left behind.

But a woman doesn't love a man
gone eighteen years, patience be damned!
I learned to love myself and lived
alone, as some might call it, manless,
supposed to weep and dream of his return.
Return? I knew that someday he might find
his way back home, that I'd be here;

yet in the interim there was no loving him,
for love is deeds, not thoughts and feelings
fluttering through the brain and blood.
What I wove on my loom I wove for me.
I dedicated every story in my threads
to bold Arachne, to all women brave enough
to spin the truth of history. At night

I smiled to hear the green and golden song
of growing skeins as I unraveled
images for the next day's telling.
Alone? When imagination looked toward dawn
as toward a secret tryst? When hands
grew daily stronger and more sure
that what they wove was powerful?

My stories broke the silence of the air
around the house, around the women
who watched them with a serious delight
and turned to one another, their eyes bright
with recognition, daring *yes*.
The suitors grew uneasy, called for wine,
insisted that the women dance for them,

and gradually as with one mind
began to shun the room where I sat weaving.
They sensed the presence there

of some new spirit—a calmness
in my smile, a way I had of gazing
at their leering faces unperturbed—
that disconcerted them, sent them away

muttering that something was amiss.
They couldn't read my loom,
saw nothing there but colors
meeting in confusion, if they looked at all.
So it went on. Years passed. I grew
older with the women, and together
we taught their daughters how to weave.

A hundred eager hands reached for the threads
and they surpassed my art so far
that I sat back in gladness knowing
silence would never still the air again.
It was that gladness, not time,
that drove the suitors wild
to claim me, shouting "Choose! Choose!"

And I would have chosen—to save us—
despite my son—had not Odysseus returned.
When he slipped into the hall in rags
and strung the bow, already I
loved him again, willed his success, welcomed
night embraces in the great carved bed.
So, loving, we continue.

And mornings, loving,
every loom a tree of light,
I weave again with the daughters around me,
fingers sure in time's glad reach,
learning from them now, faithful
to the green and golden stories
that celebrate our love.

The Feather of the Winter Owl

    for Kristen Britain

You will find it by moonstone,
the kind of light that rises up
within your breath when you dream
a long forest, a kind forest—

unless a nightmare grows sharp hooves
and kicks the path to crimson embers,
stifling soft ferns from their spiral
reach for leaf-tossed rain.

Listen: *HOO-hoo-HOO* the secret
language wings and talons know,
mice stilled in hungry forays,
moles alert in tunneled earth.

Almost cold enough for ice,
almost black enough for prayer,
your breath aching to take shape
within the branch-thick heavy air—

and then, there, a velvet white
promise of magic on dark-root moss.
What you've always heard of flight.
The way through. A grand bird's loss.

Prayer Sequence

Tie the first one to a blue balloon,
but don't let go, don't let it rise.
Like a plastic bag murdering a manatee
it could choke a bird.

Shape the second one after a tornado
has torn up all the thriving oaks
next to the teahouse a woman created.
Her black dog barked, saving her.

The third should be purple as spring dusk
on a road used by soldiers to walk to war.
Their socks have rotted. Their boots stink.
Their guns mean nothing anymore.

Pull the fourth from the mouth of a fish
like a coin spent on a Greek island.
It has touched so many travelers
its date is a poem lost in time.

Five: the last, your salvation. A girl
with a body like a painted drawer
will hand you a bone, a jeweled collar.
Bury one. Burn the other. Sing.

An Account of My Disappearances

      after Jack Anderson

1.

The day of roses.
The day of withered thorns.
With one small bag of paisley silk
I slipped into my small blue car
and drove, drove to Pennsylvania.
Shirts without buttons.
Quilts.

2.

Music gonged and hammered down the hill.
I stayed where I was.
No one saw me.

3.

The oven burned my cranberry muffins
before the priest could arrive.
I fled. New ice
shattered beneath my feet.

4.

The time of seven months.
The time I counted seagulls
like pennies in a fountain.
My mother had been dead
for many years, but still
I traveled South.

5.

Only my voice
like a nymph in a cave
ashamed of loving
a perfect man.

6.

The first time: to New York City.
With the boy I never saw again.
His name was Paul.

7.

The last one: raccoon tracks
in late Spring snow, daughter
of the one who growled and spit.
I put on my leather fox mask.
A red-winged blackbird called.

When Lilith Goes Out Dancing

       after Lauren Rinaldi's painting, "A Fall from Grace," 2015

She ties green ribbons in her long red hair
that match the eyes she likes to narrow
and widen when a partner appears
to smile and take her small pale hand.
Her skirts are emerald and at her throat
she wears a necklace of peridot
gathered from a volcano's heart
and cut to brilliance with a flaming knife.
Her partner gazes and offers roses
white and tight as the tiny fists
of the demon she's left behind at home
to watch over her sleeping baby—
the one she stole three midnights ago
who tonight will grow too fast, too soon
into a woman they'll have to kill
when Lilith returns in worn-out shoes.

End-of-Day

Where infants sleep, I gather
nets I've woven from desert grass
and whiskers of the wide-eyed lions
who hunt with me, who lie down long
in the shadows of my shoulders' wings.
My womb spewed out the world's
dark demons, but refuses me

my own warm child to cherish
in strong mother arms and name
powerfully with the seven vowels
of my tongue's alphabet. She lives
only when I dare to dream;
I wake up cold and empty.
And so I creep where babies

breathe alone in cradle beds:
I croon, I whisper, I touch the heads
descended from that dead first man
I left behind in appled Eden
for my tawny owls, my gray jackals,
my faithful beasts wild as I am
in new moon's lack of light.

Old Women Crying on the Beach

Alone, I hear them.
Walking here where waves
make tiny white-maned stallions
in the dark. Their voices carry
cadences of story I can't
comprehend but deeply feel
in the place where reason ends.

Whale song others say. *The moan
of rigging in high wind.
The inside of your own
long yearning.* And they laugh.

Walking here I almost see
the women let their hair down
in the dark to trail along
the stallions' flanks, still murmuring,
still moving me to join them
beyond tears. Who dares to say
to me they are not real?

They ride the dark. The hands
they lift from flying manes
are tipped with stars and stars.

Beneath the Tallest Live Oak

You know you are dead.
You are not dreaming; you are dead.
In a swing as bright as the moon
sits the child who fell through skyscraper glass.
In a whirlwind of ashes and bone
laughs the woman who was your mother.
You're wearing a long pink cotton dress
and a necklace of clear glass fishes.
A lizard dares to climb into your hand.
It pulses, settles, stays.

Heavenly spheres are the thousand cicadas
released from their hard monstrous husks.
You remember you were someone else
with a name, hot love, piles of books.
Here you delight in a simple chair
someone carved from very new wood.
Light lingers, palpable with sea.
Your hair is still silver and white and gray
lifted just a bit by the breeze
that pushes through pale jacaranda.

A shadow of a sharp-leafed frond
wavers beneath a rippling web
wide enough for the eye of God
to rest there, summon, glitter.
You remember a prayer you learned
and you let it shape your lips.
The lizard stirs, rises, moves
to the palm of someone else.
The small child waves to you.
You taste your mother's breath.

Acknowledgments

Chautauqua: "An Account of My Disappearances"
City Works Journal: "My Granddaughter Hands Me a Gilded Box"
Crosswinds Journal: "Beneath the Tallest Live Oak"
december: "Learning to Lie, the Nice Girl," "What He Meant, the Miller"
Delphinium: A Journal of Art and Literature: "Dark Matters"
Earth's Daughters: "Penelope"
Ellipsis: Literature and Art: "Your Mother"
Foliate Oak Literary Magazine: "End-of-Day"
The Healing Muse: "Black"
The Hollins Critic: "Leda's Sister and the Geese"
IthacaLit.com: "The Feather of the Winter Owl"
Kansas City Voices: "Autism, 1954"
Nimrod International Journal: "My Beast," "Paws"
Outlook Springs: "In His Fingers"
Oyez Review: "Sonnet"
Passager: "Prayer Sequence"
Poetry Center Anthology: "Helen"
The Poet's Touchstone: "I Will Give You Flowers"
Rosebud: "Path"
Spillway: "When Your Daughter-in-Law Hates Magic"
Steam Ticket: "Noir"
Stone Canoe: "After My Brother Stole Me Away"
Sun Star Review: "When Lilith Goes Out Dancing"
Women Artists Datebook 2018: "Blackbird Bakery"
Yankee: "Old Women Crying on the Beach," "The Women Who Write About Animals"

"When Lilith Goes Out Dancing" was included in *Art & Words 2015*, an annual mixed-media show at Art on the Boulevard, Fort Worth, TX, curated by Bonnie Stufflebeam.

Special thanks to the Poetry Society of New Hampshire for an award that helped to forward the work on this collection.

About FutureCycle Press

FutureCycle Press is dedicated to publishing lasting English-language poetry books, chapbooks, and anthologies in both print-on-demand and Kindle ebook formats. Founded in 2007 by long-time independent editor/publishers and partners Diane Kistner and Robert S. King, the press incorporated as a nonprofit in 2012. A number of our editors are distinguished poets and writers in their own right, and we have been actively involved in the small press movement going back to the early seventies.

The FutureCycle Poetry Book Prize and honorarium is awarded annually for the best full-length volume of poetry we publish in a calendar year. Introduced in 2013, our Good Works projects are anthologies devoted to issues of universal significance, with all proceeds donated to a related worthy cause. Our Selected Poems series highlights contemporary poets with a substantial body of work to their credit; with this series we strive to resurrect work that has had limited distribution and is now out of print.

We are dedicated to giving all of the authors we publish the care their work deserves, making our catalog of titles the most diverse and distinguished it can be, and paying forward any earnings to fund more great books.

We've learned a few things about independent publishing over the years. We've also evolved a unique, resilient publishing model that allows us to focus mainly on vetting and preserving for posterity poetry collections of exceptional quality without becoming overwhelmed with bookkeeping and mailing, fundraising activities, or taxing editorial and production "bubbles." To find out more about what we are doing, come see us at www.futurecycle.org.

www.ingramcontent.com/pod-product-compliance
Lightning Source LLC
Chambersburg PA
CBHW070453050426
42450CB00012B/3262